Robertson's Guide to
Field Sports in Scotland

To Robin

best wishes

Alan Robertson

Robertson's Guide to Field Sports in Scotland
ISBN 978-0-9563744-5-5
Published by Finks Publishing Ltd +44 (0)1466 700367
Written and distributed by Alastair Robertson +44 (0)1466 740331
First edition published 2013
Finks Publishing, Cairnargat, Glass, Huntly, Aberdeenshire Scotland AB54 4XA
© Alastair Robertson
www.finkspublishing.com

CRUMPET

This book is dedicated to Crumpet (aka Doodles)
and all our long gone dogs, for their loyalty,
affection and companionship.
Oh yes, and Kate my long suffering wife
who was not amused to find that
this book was being dedicated to a dog.

.

Chez Roux in Scotland
Alladale Wilderness Reserve Ardgay
The Atholl Edinburgh
Blanefield House Turnberry
Cromlix Dunblane
Greywalls Hotel Edinburgh
Inver Lodge Hotel North West Scotland
Rocpool Hotel Inverness
Rocpool Apartments Edinburgh

For further details www.icmi.co.uk

Foreword

I came to Scotland for the first time almost 50 years ago, fishing with my young family. I cannot say we caught very much. Perhaps if we had had this book we would have caught more! Who knows? We stayed in a B&B at Lochinver on our way to Skye and the children caught mackerel from the sea which we had for supper. It was my first experience of how, in Scotland the best and freshest wild produce is all around; in the rivers and sea, in the woods and on the hills. For me, fishing is a passion. To catch a fish, prepare it, cook it and serve it to family or friends is, for me, perfect. For others it will be to stalk a stag, or the excitement and camaraderie of walking with dogs for a wild pheasant. This is the natural, age-old connection between man and food. I hope this book will encourage more people to make that connection. I hope they will then discover the same satisfaction and pleasure I have had from bringing home and serving some of the finest game in the world.

Bon chance et bon appétit

 *Albert Roux OBE KFO*

Finding out about field and country sports in Scotland

There has never been any shortage of sport in Scotland. But until the **Scottish Country Sports Tourism Group (SCSTG)** appeared on the scene there was often no simple way for the visitor to find out where to go or what to do.

The new **SCSTG** website **www.countrysportsscotland.com** is designed for experts, novices and families alike. All can now:

- Browse for fishing, shooting and stalking opportunities
- Find special offers and packages, even last minute deals
- Discover field sports friendly hotels and places to stay
- See what the experts advise on equipment
- Pick up handy hints for sporting holidays

The important thing is that no one need feel afraid to ask even if they are complete novices. Scotland is brimming with people for whom field sports is a passion. They love nothing more than to pass on their experiences and tips to others. If the **SCSTG** doesn't know the answer it will know someone who does.

Who is SCSTG?

SCSTG was set up in 2004 to develop the full potential of the Scottish field sports market both at home and abroad. Its members include all the leading field sports and land-owner organisations from the worlds of fishing, shooting and stalking besides Scottish Government countryside and tourism organisations. It works closely with field sports and accommodation providers.

A world class sporting experience!

Contents

Introduction

What happens on The Glorious 12th? How do you go about stalking a real life Monarch of the Glen? What is a Macnab?

This book is for those who know nothing about stalking deer, catching salmon, or shooting grouse, but are still curious to know what it is all about. It explains who owns the rivers and land, how much and how little you can pay for a day's fishing, the role of the gamekeeper and the type of guns, dogs and the equipment in common use. It also explains the part that field sports play in the conservation of the Scottish countryside and reveals that field sports are not the exclusive preserve of the rich and famous.

'Going North, King's Cross Station', 1893 by George Earl. One of a pair of paintings showing the Victorian fashion for all things Scottish as they leave London for the summer sporting season armed with guns, rods, golf clubs and dogs. It's twin, 'Coming South, Perth Station' appears at the end of the book (p112). Both courtesy of the National Railway Museum, York.

A Brief History

Field sports in Britain had, for centuries, been the preserve of the rich and powerful. But the new railways of the 19th century were to open up Scotland to the Victorian middle classes, industrialists and wealthy entrepreneurs. They were following in the footsteps of Queen Victoria and Prince Albert who had made Scotland fashionable by buying Balmoral in 1844. Prior to the advent of railways the only comfortable way of getting to Scotland was by boat.

Now, as the railways inched further and further north, Scotland became all the rage, the place to be seen in early autumn, on the grouse moor, river or deer forest. But Scottish landowners had not initially welcomed the invasion. 'Attracted by grouse, the mansion houses of half our poor devils of Highland lairds are occupied by rich and titled southrons (southerners),' wrote the High Court Judge, Lord Cockburn. The 'poor devils' were not feeble-minded however. The 'shootings' at Glen Urquhart on Loch Ness had been let for £100 in 1836. In 1864 they were let for £2,000.

The rivers the lairds had once netted for salmon to sell were now more profitably let to sporting anglers. The hills over which they had trudged for a few grouse and mountain hares became grouse moors with lines of butts, like those of Yorkshire and Lancashire. The replacement of old muzzle loaders with breech-loading shotguns and paper cartridges had also revolutionised game shooting for grouse, pheasant and partridge. Stalking the 'Monarch of the Glen' or driving deer towards rifles became a sport for which the new sporting public was prepared to pay. Hotels sprang up in the major towns to cater for the sporting trade. New lodges were built in the hills.

Two world wars and 150 years later, the Scottish sporting traditions established by the Victorians and Edwardians survive. The ownership of estates and rivers has changed. But the hills and rivers remain for the enjoyment and wonderment of future generations regardless of income or social standing.

Who owns Scotland?

Nearly all land and rivers in Scotland are privately owned and managed, and always have been. But unlike in many countries, there is no restriction on who can buy or own land in Scotland. Some of the best Highland sporting estates are (or have been) owned by foreign nationals including Danes, Swedes, Belgians and Arabs. While Highland and Border estates can be huge, often 50,000 acres (20,200 hectares (ha)) or more, most shooting and low ground stalking will take place over privately-owned farm and woodland. In Scotland the average family-owned farm is around 250 acres (100ha).

What's it all Worth?

Shooting, game fishing and stalking are worth at least £360million a year to the Scottish economy, only marginally less than golf and more than mountain biking and kayaking. Shooting alone supports the equivalent of 11,000 full time jobs. Salmon and trout fishing support 2000 jobs and generate an estimated £120million a year. Red deer management generates an estimated 320 full-time jobs and another 460 part time jobs, while stalking as a whole is valued at £80million a year.

These are significant sums, particularly for rural areas where wages are traditionally low and jobs hard to find. Village shops, hotels, garages, pubs, even school children and students taking holiday jobs will all depend to some extent, on the money sporting visitors and their families can bring into a community. Around 400,000 people a year take part in Scottish field sports of which 150,000 will be from overseas, the remainder from Scotland and the UK.

Field Sports Fairs

The three day Scottish Game Fair held each June/July at Scone, Perthshire attracts more than 32,000 visitors a year. The Highland Field Sports Fair at Moy near Inverness on the first Friday/Saturday in August attracts 15,000 visitors annually. Gordon Castle at Fochabers, Moray holds a country fair and Highland games each May.

Field Sports, Conservation and the Landscape

There is now abundant evidence that where land is managed for the benefit of game, small birds, particularly waders, will flourish. The same is true of rivers and lochs. The shooting industry alone spends an estimated £43million a year on habitat improvement and wildlife management, from planting woodland to creating wetlands for wildfowl. River trusts and boards have opened up 2,186km of previously blocked rivers and spent more than £5million on improvements to the river bed and bank management. Consequently, survey after survey shows that the Scottish landscape is a key factor in attracting 16 million visitors a year, – a landscape moulded by the demands of field sports. Without field sports and the conservation work needed to create and maintain wildlife habitats there would be little to shoot or catch – and fewer visitors. Wildlife Estates Scotland, an accreditation scheme promoting good management practice, has been launched to highlight conservation benefits.

More than half of Scotland is managed with field sports in mind. Out of a total land mass of 19,275,000million acres (7.8million ha), the management of 10,870,000 million acres (4.4million ha) are influenced by shooting alone. In all, 1,730,000 million acres (0.7million ha) are managed directly with shooting in mind.

Field Sports or Country Sports? What's the difference?

It is a matter of choice which you use. Field sports is the traditional term for hunting, shooting, fishing and stalking. Country Sports is a more modern term.

The Game & Wildlife Conservation Trust (GWCT)

The science-based charity has been researching and developing game and wildlife management techniques for more than 75 years. It has a strong presence in Scotland and collaborates with the Scottish Government and other wildlife organisations including the RSPB. It hosts the annual Scottish Game Fair at Scone Palace, Perth each June. *www.gwct.org.uk*

Stalker, ghillie, gamekeeper – what's the difference?

There is no hard and fast rule that can distinguish between the three. A gamekeeper is employed to make sure there is plenty of game to shoot. But depending on the time of year, a keeper may also help out on the river or during a deer cull. Ghillie is Gaelic for servant. It usually refers to someone who works on the river helping anglers catch and land fish. A stalker will be employed mainly in deer management. He or she may also be referred to as  a ghillie along with the pony boy or ghillie who helps with the pony or 'Argo'. A stalker may well take guests fishing or help with gamekeeping.

Are there any women gamekeepers, stalkers or ghillies?
Very few if any. Consequently it is hard to explain why not. But these are not very sociable jobs out of season, often in remote areas and under harsh conditions. Perhaps men are just better suited.

Can you learn to be a gamekeeper?
There are certified gamekeeping and deer management courses in Scotland: North Highland College, Thurso, Caithness *www.northhighland.uhi.ac.uk*
Elmwood College, Cupar, Fife *www.elmwood.ac.uk*
Borders College, St Boswells *www.borderscollege.ac.uk*
Oatridge College, West Lothian *www.oatridge.ac.uk* provides countryside and environmental management courses
Barony College, Dumfriesshire *www.barony.ac.uk* specialises in fisheries management training.

The Language of Field Sports

Field sports has its own language and words. Where a word or phrase is particular to the sport it appears here in quotation marks. For instance 'guns' not only means shotguns but those people carrying guns and shooting.

There is a natural confusion between those who speak Anglo-English, even with a Scottish accent, and those who speak American-English. In Britain and Scotland 'shooting' refers to the pursuit of birds or animals with a shotgun. In the US this is called 'hunting' and includes shooting deer which in Britain is referred to as 'stalking'. In English, 'hunting' generally means the pursuit of foxes with hounds and horses or on foot.

A reminder...

The game laws in Scotland are not the same as those in England, Wales and Northern Ireland. Scotland has its own legal system. For instance in Scotland you do not need a permit to fish but you  must have permission from the owner of the fishing or their agent. The dates for closed seasons, the times when you may not shoot, fish or stalk, are also different in Scotland to the rest of the UK. The Republic of Ireland also has its own rules and regulations.

MURDO MCLEOD www.murdophoto.com

Dressed to kilt (above): This party at Balavil Estate (www.balavil.com) on Speyside has dressed up for the first day of the grouse shooting season, August 12th – 'The Glorious Twelfth'.

Blooding

Blooding rituals occur all over the world and probably go back thousands if not millions of years to man's primal beginnings. The blood of a dead animal or bird is smeared on the face of the 'hunter' after his or her first 'kill'. Whether this gives us the expression 'first blood,' is uncertain. In Scotland this is usually the blood of a deer or grouse, but can be any 'first'. In fox hunting the blood of the fox would be smeared on a young rider's face. There is no age restriction on blooding.

KIRSTEN SCHEUERL www.kirstenscheuerl.com

What is a Macnab?

A 'Macnab' is one of the most demanding personal challenges in sport. To kill a stag, catch a salmon and shoot a brace (a pair) of grouse in one day takes planning and skill. The feat takes its name from the book John Macnab, the story of three well-to-do Edwardian gents poaching in the Highlands. But what gave John Buchan the idea for a novel which in turn spawned a sporting challenge?

The real-life John Macnab

John Buchan based his story on an incident in the life of Lt James Brander-Dunbar of Pitgaveny, near Elgin in Moray. Dining with fellow officers of the 3rd Cameron Highlanders in Inverness he complained that no-one had asked him stalking that autumn of 1897. Instead, he would have to take to poaching. 'I could kill a beast in any forest in Scotland.' he boasted. The 4th Lord Abinger took up the challenge and bet Brander-Dunbar (right) he could not poach a stag from his 40,000 acre Inverlochy estate near Fort William. The bet made, Dunbar secretly lodged at Keppoch across the River Spean from Inverlochy. On the third morning he spotted a stag which in the dawn half light mistook him as a rival for its hinds, and advanced, '... muttering right into my face

A gun bags his brace of grouse on Gannochy Estate,
Angus to complete a Macnab.

presenting an easy breast-on shot.' At the sound of the shot Abinger's
men almost immediately appeared. Reading the lie of the land, Brander-
Dunbar evaded his pursuers and worked his way to safety dragging his
.303 rifle and the severed head of the stag back across the Spean. That
afternoon he took the head up to Inverlochy which is now a five star
hotel, to receive a cheque for £20 made out to 'J.B.Dunbar, poacher'.
In one version he sent the stag's testicles up to the castle with the
postman. The story was picked up by John Buchan who embellished the
tale and published John Macnab in 1925. Brander-Dunbar became a
soldier, guerrilla fighter in the Boer War and big game hunter in Africa.
At Pitgaveny he delighted in showing visitors his coffin inscribed with
the words 'A fine natural blackguard'. By the time he died aged 95 in
1969 he was reputed to have fathered 19 illegitimate children.

Shooting

Scotland is a country rich in every sort of game - grouse, pheasants, duck, geese, partridge, woodcock and snipe. There are hares in the hills and fields and the woods are home to flocks of wild woodpigeons. There is no legal limit to the number of birds or animals you may shoot over any period of time.

What you can shoot

- Game
    - Red Grouse
    - Pheasant
    - Partridge
    - Ptarmigan (mountain grouse)
    - Black Grouse (woodland grouse)
    - Coot and Moorhen (seldom shot)
    - Golden Plover
    - Woodcock
    - Snipe
    - Hare
    - Geese
    - Duck

CALUM CAMPBELL

- You may also shoot rabbits and pigeons which do not count as game, but require to be controlled to prevent crop damage.

www.gwct.org.uk

Open seasons – when you can shoot game

Game has open and close seasons – periods during which it may not be shot. This is to ensure birds and animals can breed and populations have time to recover from hostile weather conditions (see list). Rabbits and woodpigeon are considered pests and can be shot all year round.

Pheasant	1 Oct – 1 Feb
Grey Partridge	1 Sept – 1Feb
Red-Legged Partridge	1 Sept – 1 Feb
Red Grouse	12 Aug – 10 Dec
Black Grouse	20 Aug – 10 Dec
Ptarmigan	12 Aug – 10 Dec
Duck/Geese (inland)	1 Sept – 31 Jan
Duck/Geese (below High Water Mark)	1 Sept – 20 Feb
Common Snipe	12 Aug – 31 Jan
Woodcock	1 Sept – 31 Jan
Brown Hare	1st Oct – 31st Jan
Mountain Hare	1st Aug – 28th/29th Feb

The role of the gamekeeper

Gamekeepers ensure game is plentiful. They control pests, rear game birds but not grouse, organise beaters and dog handlers, and decide the best way to run each day's shooting. They are employed by, and work closely with, the owner of the shoot or the shooting tenant. Large estates may employ under keepers and trainees. On grouse moors, keepers also have to know where the birds are most likely to be found over thousands of acres. Keepers must also keep a look out for poachers, particularly gangs looking for deer. It will cost anything between £30,000 and £50,000 a year to employ a keeper when expenses such as house, fuel, vehicles, clothing, dogs and ammunition are taken into consideration.

KIRSTEN SCHEUERL www.kirstenscheuerl.com

Types of Shooting

Shooting either takes place on a 'rough shoot' – a few people walking with guns and dogs – or on a formal, 'driven shoot' with beaters flushing birds over a line of 'guns'. 'Flighting', or waiting for duck or geese to come in to land, is popular. Woodpigeons are plentiful in farmland areas. Clay pigeons (targets) are also popular with those who enjoy shooting but may not have the opportunity, or inclination, to shoot live birds and animals.

Rough shooting

Rough shooting along with the pigeon shooting, is the most popular of all wild game field sports. One or more people, usually informally dressed, walk with dogs along hedgerows, ditches, fields and woods. Syndicates (groups) of friends, often rent land from farmers or estates for a few pounds or even a bottle of whisky at Christmas! They may 'put down' (release) a few reared pheasants and control the pests themselves. A day's 'bag' could be a few pheasants, rabbit, woodcock and pigeon. Or even nothing!

Driven shooting *pheasants and partridges (also see grouse section)*

These are more formal affairs when 'guns' tend to dress smartly. Shoots take place over countryside, woods and fields managed for agriculture as well as shooting. The pheasants or partridges are reared by game keepers over the summer and released into the wild before the shooting season. Ten or more beaters and keepers with dogs walk in line to flush out game and 'drive' the birds towards a line of 6-10 'guns' standing 50-60m apart. There may be four 'drives' before lunch and two afterwards. Dogs handled by 'pickers up' retrieve dead or wounded birds that fall behind the line of guns.

The most common driven shooting is for pheasants with bags from 50-400. Duck, woodcock and pigeon may also be in the bag. Each gun will be given a choice of between two and four head of game to take home. The rest will be sold to a game dealer. A high proportion of processed British game is exported. Driven grouse is the most expensive and exclusive form of driven shooting (see grouse).

Wildfowling

Scotland is home to more than 700,000 migrating geese from Iceland, Spitzbergen and Greenland. They spend the winter on estuaries and lochs down the east and west coasts. Wildfowling in Scotland falls into two categories - inland and foreshore

Inland goose shooting near the coast is the most popular. The geese are lured within shot of the hidden 'guns' with life-size decoys as they come into feed on stubble or grass in the early morning. Professional geese guides take out parties. Shooting on the foreshore (estuaries and coastal marshes below the level of the high tide) is a more specialist sport and not for the faint-hearted. It needs stamina and patience to wait for duck or geese in wet, muddy and often cold, dark, conditions during winter. You need a good dog and you also need to know the tides. The inexperienced can easily be cut off or lost in fog. A 12-bore is normally used with large No 3 shot for geese and smaller No 4-6 for duck and teal. In Scotland, unlike England, you must use non-toxic shot, like steel, not lead, over wetlands.

What you can shoot

- **Duck** – mallard, Teal, Wigeon, Pintail, Tufted duck, Pochard, Shoveller, Goldeneye, Gadwall.
- **Geese** – Pink-footed, Greylag, Canada.
- **Waders** – Golden plover.
- **Others** – Woodcock, Snipe. Coot and Moorhen are rarely shot today.

It is illegal to sell a wild goose. This is a conservation/anti-poaching measure. They may not be shot on Sundays or Christmas Day.

Pigeon shooting

This is the most popular and accessible of all forms of shooting. Pigeons are an agricultural pest. Farmers are often happy to allow shooting over crops or stubble in late summer. Pigeons are ideal quarry for learners of all ages. Decoys are widely used to lure them into a field. Pigeons can also be 'flighted' in the evening as they come in to woods to roost. Goose guides with farming contacts also take out parties for pigeon shooting. Most calibres of shotgun are suitable. Pests or 'vermin' can be shot on Sundays, but few do.

www.gwct.org.uk

Hare

There are two types of hare in Scotland, the brown hare which lives on arable land and the smaller blue or mountain hare. The brown hare, due largely to modern agricultural practice, has been in decline. The mountain hare which turns white in winter with the snow lives on the bare hills. Numbers vary hugely from area to area.

Fox 'lamping'

A number of sporting agents arrange 'lamping' expeditions at night. The fox is lured into rifle range and the beam of a spotlight either by a fox call or a 'squeak' made by hand and mouth that sounds like a distressed rabbit.

Rabbits

Ferreting is an age old method of controlling rabbits. A ferret, put into a warren, will bolt rabbits into nets stretched over holes or into the open for waiting guns. Sporting agents may be able to arrange expeditions.

Who can Shoot

Anyone of any nationality can shoot, providing they have permission of the land owner, and satisfy legal requirements. There are two types of certificate: a shotgun certificate and a firearms certificate. A shotgun certificate is for shotguns only and a firearms certificate for rifles only. They are not interchangeable. Anyone who owns a gun must have a certificate issued by police who first make background checks. There is no limit to the number of guns a person may own. There is no minimum age for applying for a shotgun certificate in the UK. However, you must be 14 before applying for a firearms (rifle) certificate. You may borrow a shotgun without a certificate for use on private land with the permission of the owner in his or her presence. In the case of a rifle you must be 17 and the lender over 18. Overseas visitors bringing guns to Scotland must apply for a temporary licence at least four weeks in advance. Sporting agents can usually deal with an application. No national permit to shoot game is required nor are there checks on ability to use a gun. In 2011, there were 71,860 rifles in Scotland and 138,939 shotguns. See **www.basc.org.uk**

Tipping the keeper

A head keeper is traditionally tipped at the end of the day. By 2012 the irregular rule of thumb was £30 per 100 birds shot. But if it has been an enjoyable day £40 should suffice regardless of the bag. For grouse anything from £50 to £100 will do. Tipping is done by concealing the notes in the palm when shaking hands to say goodbye, while being presented with a brace or two of birds to take home in the other hand. Ostentatiously shoving £50 notes into the keepers top pocket is very un-British, although the keeper won't complain.

CHARLES SAINSBURY-PLAICE

Guns

Game birds and ground game in Scotland are shot with shotguns of the appropriate calibre. Deer are shot with rifles. A shotgun is for small game that flies or runs.

Shotguns

Most shotguns are double barrelled with barrels arranged either side-by-side or one on top of the other – known as an 'over and under'. Which you use is entirely a matter of personal preference. These days most guns will automatically 'eject' the used cartridges when the gun is opened after firing. Semi automatic shotguns are legally restricted to three shots. They are used for wildfowling and pest control, ie. pigeons and rabbits, but not game like pheasants or grouse.

Shotgun sizes are measured in bore in the UK known as gauge in the US. The smaller the number, the larger the gun, so a 12-bore will have a greater number of pellets and spread of shot than a smaller 28-bore. The range will be about the same.

- The most popular size is the **12-bore**, an all-rounder powerful enough for all game shooting in Scotland including geese.
- The **16-bore** has largely fallen out of fashion.
- The **20-bore** is slightly smaller and requires greater accuracy. It is widely favoured by women and those who want or need something lighter than a 12-bore but which can still bring down a pheasant.
- The **28-bore** is lighter again and requires even greater accuracy. Often a first or second gun for young learners. But used by expert shots to give themselves a greater challenge.
- The **Four Ten (.410)**, often a first gun for learners, and frequently single-barrelled non-ejector. Deadly if accurate.

Who makes the best shotguns?

It's very much a matter of opinion! James Purdey, Holland and Holland and Boss are considered among the best. Prices for a new Purdey side-by-side 12-bore start at around £60,000. However, the Beretta Silver Pigeon under-and-over 12 or 20-bore is among the best value for money at £1,500.

Scottish gunsmiths are highly-rated and include David McKay Brown and Dickson & MacNaughton. A Mackay Brown 12-bore will cost about £27,000 before engraving.

GAVIN GARDINER LTD

Crocodile Gun: Intricate engraving by Aberfeldy-based Malcolm Appleby who engraves guns for Holland and Holland and the Royal Armouries. His engraved Mackay Brown 12-bore sold for £40,000.

History of bores

Guns sizes go back to the days of cannon. The bore of a gun is dictated by the number of lead balls the same diameter as the gun barrel that it takes to make up 1lb in weight. So if there are 12 balls to the lb the gun will be a 12-bore. In the case of the smaller 28-bore there will be 28 balls to the lb. And so on. The odd one out is the Four Ten which is .410 of an inch in diameter. Cartridges come with different 'loads' and shot sizes. Large No 4 shot is suitable for ducks and geese. A 30gms load of No 5 or No 6 shot covers most eventualities.

Art and Field Sports

Field sports have been a popular subject for artists from the days of cave drawings. Artists like Archibald Thorburn (1860-1935) depicted not only game birds and animals but shooting expeditions. The richly detailed paintings of game birds by artists such as Rodger McPhail are hugely popular with field sports enthusiasts.

Above: Red-legged partridges by Claire Harkess www.claireharkess.com

What it costs

Driven pheasants

The price for driven pheasants is calculated on the expectation of how many birds will be shot. The final price may vary depending on the final bag. In 2012, pheasants were being valued for letting purposes at around £30 each. Thus a 200 bird day would cost £6,000 plus VAT which divided between eight guns is £900 per gun.

Walked up

A rented day's organised rough shooting will cost around £150 per gun. The bag will vary. A game dealer will pay between 25p and 50p per bird depending on condition and the time of year.

Dogs

Shooting dogs generally fall into three categories in Scotland: spaniels, retrievers and pointers. And keepers use terriers for fox control.

Spaniel
The ideal all round gun dog. There are two distinct types, the heavier Springer and the smaller Working Cocker, not to be confused with the Show or American Cocker. Spaniels are small, tough and inexhaustible, ideal for flushing out and finding game in small crevices and thickets.

Labrador/Retriever
Black and golden Labradors are among the most popular gundogs in Britain, good at 'marking' (spotting) shot birds and retrieving them. The longer haired Golden Retriever was originally developed to retrieve ducks. All retrievers are good swimmers and very good natured – usually.

Pointers
Pointers and setters stalk their prey by smell and then 'point' with their noses. They are used specially for sniffing out grouse. The German shorthaired pointers, the Vizslas and Weimaraners are increasingly popular as all round shooting dogs.

Dogs are vital for flushing live game and finding dead birds.
Clockwise from top left, opposite German shorthaired pointer, Golden Retriever, Black Labrador, Working Cocker Spaniel and Weimaraners.

Grouse

Grouse deserve a special section to themselves. The Red Grouse (*Lagopus lagopus scoticus*) is unique to the British Isles and particularly associated with Scotland. The opening day of the season, August 12th, is known as 'The Glorious Twelfth'. Grouse are completely wild and cannot be reared, unlike partridge or pheasant. To shoot driven grouse in Scotland is considered the ultimate wild game shooting experience. Not only are grouse the size of a small wood pigeon, they are unpredictable. They fly fast and low, (or fast and high!) at up to 90mph in groups known as 'coveys' and can break, twist or turn in any direction. They live on fresh heather shoots and insects in some of the most exposed terrain in Europe. It's a wonder they survive at all. Grouse are prone to tick-born Louping Ill Disease, bad weather in the spring, foxes, ravens and raptors. Some years owners have to cancel all shooting because of low numbers and let the stocks recover naturally.

Oops...

Safety pep talks are compulsory on all shoots and safety sticks on either side of butts can prevent 'guns' swinging 'through the line'. All the same, as grouse can fly incredibly low and fast between butts, accidents are not infrequent. The chairman of Sotheby's, the international auction house, had 60 pellets removed

from his face and arms after he was shot on a moor in Yorkshire during 2012. A British Home Secretary Lord Whitelaw famously 'peppered' a neighbour when he swung 'through the line' of butts. The great Duke of Wellington, a notoriously bad shot, famously bagged Lord Granville, a beater and a washerwoman. These days a horn sounds to warn 'guns' that beaters are approaching.

How big is a grouse moor?

There is no hard and fast rule. Some areas will 'hold' grouse better than others so a moor could be anything from a thousand acres to 60,000 acres. Estates often split their moors into 'beats' for practical management purposes and shoot different beats on different days.

How much does it cost to shoot grouse

The cost is calculated on the number of 'brace' (pair) shot. A brace of driven grouse in 2012 was valued at around £150. Therefore a 200-brace-day will cost £30,000 plus VAT. For eight 'guns' the day will cost £4,500 each. 'Walked up' grouse costs almost half at around £70-£80 a brace. The birds remain the property of the shoot (guns will be given a brace or two to take home).

Where is the best grouse shooting

In Scotland, The Borders, Angus, Deeside and Donside in Aberdeenshire and Moray. The Highlands is possibly the least good grouse area because of the terrain. But even these estates can produce 800 brace or more a year.

Why is grouse shooting so expensive?

It's the cost of maintaining a moor. An owner, or tenant will need to employ at least two keepers and pay for their housing and vehicles. Contractors will be needed for fencing and remaking hill tracks. Seasonal staff, cooks and beaters need hiring. Don't expect any change at 2012 prices out of £120,000 a year and much more if you own a lodge which will need staff and maintenance. And some years there will be nothing to shoot because grouse are wild, unpredictable and prone to disease. No grouse, no income. Owning or renting a grouse moor is a hobby, a passion, and you don't expect to make money.

What does a grouse cost?

An estate will sell grouse at around £5 a brace to a game dealer. Sometimes chefs and hotels have their own arrangements with individual estates. (Rules, the London restaurant, owns its own estate.) A dealer will sell them on at around £12 a brace, plucked clean and oven ready. Expect to pay from £7.50 to £13 online per SINGLE oven ready bird. Restaurants will charge anything from £20.

Can I buy a Scottish grouse moor and how much will it cost?

You will need to join the queue. At any given time there will be around 20 home and overseas buyers looking for a grouse moor. The value is calculated on the average number of birds shot over a five and 10 year period. In 2011, a single brace, or pair, of grouse were valued at £5,000. The same year five moors in Scotland sold for just under £5million each and one, exceptionally, for £20million.

Long leases on moors are increasingly common. You can rent a run down moor for a peppercorn rent over 20-25 years for the enjoyment of bringing it back to life and, if you are very lucky, enjoy some good years shooting. You will have to pay for keepers and all upkeep and then hand it back to the owner at the end of the lease. Expect to pay £120,000 a year upkeep and more to begin with.

Heather burning - muirburn

The patchwork of strips on Scotland's moorland is the result of burning heather. Burning is the natural method of rejuvenating old heather to produce the fresh new shoots on which grouse feed. Muirburn also creates areas of heather each at different stages of growth which provide nesting habitat for a wide variety of birds, besides grouse. By law, and to minimise the risk to ground nesting birds, managed burning may take place only between October 1 and 30th April, in accordance with the Muirburn Code.

Grouse Shooting

There are two ways of shooting grouse: 'driven' (the expensive way) and 'walked up' (the less expensive way).

Driven grouse

Once up on the moor, which may take an hour in 4x4 vehicles, the 'guns' – normally 8-10 – will each go to their respective butt. Butts are permanent hides, usually made of stone and peat half dug into the moor. They can often be seen from roads crossing moorland. Butts are usually 30-40 metres apart. If it is a 'double-gun' day each 'gun' will have a loader in the butt who will reload one gun while the other is being fired. Only moors with a very good stock of grouse are able to shoot double guns. Most shoot single guns. Beaters (often students and East Europeans) and keepers with dogs will have started walking towards the butts from up to two miles away, flushing or 'driving' the birds in front of them towards the 'guns'. When the beaters get within gunshot a horn is blown to warn guns not to shoot in front. Pickers up with dogs will be standing well behind the butts to pick up shot birds, unless 'guns' have their own dogs which they are usually keen to 'work'. The keeper's dogs will pick any grouse in front.

Walking up and shooting over dogs

Walking up is the original, some would say 'natural' way of shooting grouse. A party of guns and beaters with dogs walk in line across the moor. Birds will fly forward to be retrieved by dogs if shot. Marking the spot where a bird falls is vital. Walking up is often a day for family and to mark August 12, the opening day of the grouse season. It will include a huge picnic lunch on the hill, but it is hard walking. Expect to walk up to five miles. Bags can vary from nothing to several dozen brace. Shooting over dogs is slightly different. 'Pointers' quarter the ground until they pick up the scent of grouse, stop and 'point'. The guns come up quietly and on a signal the dogs flush the birds.

www.gwct.org

Partridges

Grouse numbers are so unpredictable that some moor owners introduced Red-legged or French partridges as an alternative source of income to help pay for the grouse moor upkeep. Red-legged can be reared like pheasants and released in late summer on the high edges of grouse moors. 'Guns' will be positioned below in gullies and valleys. The birds, smaller than grouse flying fast and dead straight, are driven over the guns – at high speed. Pheasant shoots often breed some partridges for suitable drives. Red-legged were probably introduced to the UK from France by Charles II in the 17th century.

The native Grey partridges which, unlike the Red-legged, fly in 'coveys' (groups) are currently under threat from changes in farming practices. They are found in arable low ground areas of Britain mainly on the flatter east coast. They can be reared but it is not easy. If numbers allow they are usually shot over stubble in autumn.

Where can you see grouse ?

Grouse are very well camouflaged and live high in the heather moors. They can be seen most of the year from any of the public roads that cross the moorland. They will occasionally pop up on walls or in laybys. Shooting takes place between August and November so walkers should keep dogs on leads. Grouse have a distinctive cry which is often said to sound like 'Go back, go back'! They fly low, hugging the contours of the ground. Like all wild birds they don't move unless they have to, either to find food, mate or to escape from predators – hen harriers, foxes, ravens, hoodie crows, weasels.

Look out for lines of grouse butts and the patchwork patterns of burnt heather. Grouse will not be far away. The birds are often best seen in winter, black against the snow picking at heather shoots, or in huge packs of up to 500 flying from one area to another in search of food.

One of the best routes for seeing grouse and Red deer is the A93, road from Blairgowrie to Ballater through Glenshee; then the A939 Ballater to Grantown-on-Spey over the Lecht. From Grantown the A939 continues over Dava Moor to Nairn with a branch off to Forres on the A940. The B974 from Fettercairn to Banchory via Cairn o'Mount crosses spectacular moors as does the A889 between Dalwhinnie on the A9 and Laggan on the A86.

Shooting Etiquette

Etiquette out shooting is the same as anywhere else – good manners and common sense.

- Do not turn up to a formal shoot in camouflage with a semi-automatic. You look like a poacher or one of the beaters.
- Don't be late and keep everyone waiting. If a shoot starts at 9.30am get there by 9.15am but not earlier than 9am.
- The blatant shooting of birds in front of your neighbour ('poaching') is not on unless you know them very well.
- Do not, unless told to, blaze away at pigeons before a pheasant drive, it alarms the birds and upsets the host/keeper.
- Don't boast how many you have shot, it's bad form. Be seen to be brilliant or happily hopeless, but keen.
- Don't take pet dogs unless they are at least semi-trained or on a lead. Shouting makes things worse.
- It's not sporting to shoot a low bird. If in doubt, leave it out.
- Safety is taken seriously and standards are high. Guns who are a danger to others are asked to leave.

What to Wear

Anything goes for rough shooting, wildfowling or waiting for pigeons. For everything else, keep warm and dry, keep colours muted – dull greens, greys or browns – and keep it lightweight. A peaked hat, like a tweed cap or 'bonnet' is important as camouflage and to keep the sun or rain out of your eyes. Insulated leather or rubber wellies are fine for winter. Lace-up walking boots with gaiters keep heather twigs out of socks on grouse moors, although wellies will do. Those who own their own shoots can wear what they like and often do, usually made in estate tweed. Otherwise, tweed, cord, moleskin 'breeks' or breeches or plus-fours, with a plain shooting jacket are fine. 'Cammo' or camouflage hats and jackets are for rough shooting. Don't be tempted by the latest technology or fashion until it has been well proven.

Estate tweeds

Many larger or older estates with keepers have their own tweed in the same way clans have tartans. Estates will have bolts of tweed woven to their own designs and made up into plus four suits for keepers, ghillies and the owner's family. Although some appear garish, they are effective camouflage on the hill. One of the first things Prince Albert did when he arrived at Balmoral with Queen Victoria was to design Balmoral tweed in a distinctive military field grey. See *Scottish Estate Tweeds*, Johnstons of Elgin (ISBN 0952532905).

Estate tweeds, like those who wear them, come in many hues, shapes and sizes.

The Female Touch

Diana was the Roman goddess of hunting. Traditionally, however, it is men who are the hunters. Yet women have proved every bit as capable as men on the shooting field.

Women often cannot really see the point of shooting game, particularly driven pheasants. Most, who do not have shooting husbands, brothers or fathers, can think of better things to do with their time and money. On the other hand they are seldom averse to a good walk. And there is often a hugely enjoyable social side to shooting; travelling to friends, overnight stays, dogs, families, children and new places to visit. And lots of fresh air. And after all the Duchess of Cambridge has been photographed shooting pheasants at Balmoral, and she owns a fashionable Working Cocker spaniel.

Women are more likely to be found on the clay pigeon range than in the butts on a grouse moor or tramping through a field of neeps (turnips). Clay pigeon shooting is after all a sport of skill which can be pursued in one's own time, in comparative comfort on a club or shooting school range with friends of one's own choosing – rather than your husband's or boyfriend's. There is no need to kill anything and you are allowed to be competitive which, in Britain at any rate, is rather frowned upon when shooting live game. Most organised shoots have a complement of women dog handlers – pickers up and beaters. Women are top breeders of field trial champions and working dogs. Dog handling requires dedication and patience. It also has a practical aspect, not simply flushing out birds but quickly finding any wounded 'runners'.

What to wear

What to wear, especially in Scotland, is a constant battle. You never quite know what the weather is going to do next. August can be roasting on the grouse moor and freezing in the river. October can be as cold as January.

The word is 'changeable' – especially in the West Highlands – so be prepared. Be practical rather than fashionable. But if you can be practical as well as fashionable, you've cracked it. It's better to go on a sporting expedition with too much clothing than too little. You can always take it off. The House of Bruar and Johnston's of Elgin specialise in sensible but well-cut gear.

It is perfectly possible to cut a dash without looking like Bibendum especially if spectating rather than participating. A fur hat, particularly a real fur hat, is terrific for winter days. But the full length Dr Zhivago look will be a hindrance if barbed wire fences have to be crossed.

If you are shooting in the winter ideally

'Pickers up' are a vital component of any driven shoot. Dogs are trained to hunt for dead or wounded birds falling behind the "guns". Women are frequently excellent and patient trainers.

you need a real shooting jacket which allows for plenty of movement. Tailored tweed jackets are great for looks and going to the game fair. But unless they are roomy and can be buttoned up to the neck - forget it. Leather coats and jackets can be stunning and smart.

Cheerful but not garish tweed trousers tucked inside boots are warm and less trouble than the traditional knee breeches. They are also fashionable. But either will do. Tweed or tartan knee length or longer skirts are perfectly acceptable. Dubarry-style leather boots are ideal footwear as are any of the insulated wellingtons made by le Chameau or Hunter. Walking boots, preferably high ones with gaiters, are best for walking any distance, although modern wellies can be good enough. Mittens are a must if you are shooting. But get the ones which convert into gloves so at least one hand will be warm.

Raptors – a Sporting Conflict

Raptors, or birds of prey, have been a source of regrettable conflict for decades between field sport interests and bird lovers. The main focus in moorland areas has been on hen harriers whose diet includes grouse. There is a widely held view that the lack of hen harriers in grouse moor areas is almost certainly due to illegal persecution in the form of deliberate disturbance of nests or actual killing of the birds. However, long-term experiments suggest that predation can be reduced through 'diversionary feeding' where dead rats and day-old chicks are put out for the birds to eat and to feed their chicks on. Translocation, the moving of birds to areas where they have no economic impact, is also under discussion. All the same, Scotland is home to almost the entire UK and Isle of Man breeding population of hen harriers Golden Eagles are also occasionally found dead – usually as a result of illegal poisoning. Buzzards which are the commonest bird of prey have made a remarkable recovery from near extinction and some appear to have turned to raiding pheasant pens.

BILL BOULTON

Getting Started

Almost all shooting starts with friends, family or acquaintances owning, renting or borrowing land as a shooting 'syndicate'. It may be a few acres of 'rough shooting' to walk around after the odd pheasant, duck, pigeon or rabbit. Or it may be an established shoot that rears its own game which is looking for new members. Shooting is a chance to get out into the country with friends and, with luck, satisfy what is left of man's hunter/gatherer instinct.

Beating

One of the best and most enjoyable ways to find out what goes on is to become a beater on pheasant or grouse shoots, flushing birds towards the 'guns'. You will be paid between £10 and £50 a day. Steady, biddable dogs are usually welcome. Ask around for the names of local gamekeepers who do the hiring. Once you are hooked into the network it's up to you. Pheasant beating is fairly easy going and takes place most Saturdays and up to four days a week on some shoots from October to February. Beating for grouse is hard work but the pay is better. Some estates hire for the season and provide hostel accommodation. The National Organisation of Beaters and Pickers Up finds beaters for shoots and vice versa *www.nobs.org.uk*

Clay pigeon clubs

Clay pigeon shooting is a huge sport which unlike game shooting happens all year round. A great many clay enthusiasts also shoot game. A clay pigeon club or range is usually a good place to meet others who may already have game shooting contacts or experience. For clubs try The Scottish Clay Target Association. *www.scta.co.uk*

Simulated shoots take place in the countryside and are the same as shooting live game except the targets are clay pigeons coming from all directions just like the real thing. Look up 'simulated shoots'.

Renting shooting

The internet is full of companies, estates and agents offering to lay on shooting. The choice is huge, from £50 a day to thousands, from pigeons to duck, to partridges and grouse. Renting farm and woodland for rough shooting can cost around £1 per acre per year. Leading agents include CKDGalbraith, *www.ckdgalbraith.co.uk* who specialise in sporting lets. Guns on Pegs advertise shooting days available all over Britain. *www.gunsonpegs. com*. The Scottish Country Sports Tourism Group is a vital link to all field sports *www.countrysportscotland.com*. The British Association for Shooting and Conservation handles all questions on guns and quarry *www.basc.org.uk*.

Fishing

Robert Burns famously wrote 'whisky and freedom go together'. The same can be said of Scotland and Salmon. But there is more to Scotland's rivers than Salmon alone. There are Brown trout in the hill lochs and their hard-fighting first cousin the quicksilver Sea trout to be caught in the gloamin'.

What you can fish for in Scotland

The main game species in Scotland are Salmon, Sea trout and Brown trout. Salmon and Sea trout migrate to the sea and return to spawn. Brown trout are resident all year round in rivers and lochs. Also: Grayling, a member of the Salmon family occur in rivers in the south of Scotland and can be caught on a fly. Pike are plentiful in lochs but come under the heading of coarse fishing. Fanatics fish for Artic Char, an Ice Age fish that became landlocked in lochs.

Where can I fish?

In almost any Scottish river or loch provided you have permission – usually from the owner or tenant who could be a farmer, estate owner, hotel or local angling association.

When can I do it?

The Salmon fishing season, which includes Sea trout, varies from river to river, opening as early as January 15 (the Tay) and closing as late as November 30 (Tweed). Sea trout arrive later than Salmon in June or July. The season for Brown trout runs from Mid-March to the end of September but varies from region-to-region. Rainbow trout fisheries are open all the year round. Grayling Char and Pike can be caught all year.

Who can fish for salmon and trout?

Unlike England or Wales no rod permit is required in Scotland. Anyone can fish for anything providing they have permission. The golden rule is: ask first. Each Salmon river and its catchment area has its own rules for the types of tackle that can be used and under what conditions. The owner of fishing may also impose their own conditions. There will also be local guidelines on the size and number of fish that can be killed and kept. It is illegal to fish for Salmon or Sea trout in Scotland on a Sunday although you can shoot as many pheasants and game as you like – but no one does.

Which are the best Salmon rivers?

The 'Big Four', the Premier Division of Scottish Salmon rivers are: Tweed, the Tay, the Dee and the Spey. (Tweed is traditionally referred to as Tweed, not 'the' Tweed! There is no reason.) There are dozens of less well known but very productive rivers. The best salmon rivers tend to be on the East Coast from Thurso in Caithness down to Tweed on the Scottish/ English border. They include the Helmsdale, Findhorn, Deveron, Don

and South and North Esks. There are hundreds of small and very productive spate rivers all up the West Coast. But some Salmon and Sea trout fishing on the West may have been affected by lice from the growing number of salmon fish farms (see fish farming, p68). Some of the best wild Brown trout fishing can be found on remote Highland lochs.

But isn't Salmon fishing very exclusive?

Yes and no. Rivers historically belonged to the large landowners, or lairds, so Salmon fishing has long been associated with the land-owning classes in Britain. The Dukes of Roxburghe, Buccleuch and Westminster for instance have extensive Salmon fishings. But few landowners keep their fishing to themselves. Most let it out to pay for the ghillies and upkeep. So the person renting fishing may be a postman or a high court judge.

Isn't it very expensive?

Not necessarily. The best beats (stretches) on the best rivers will be the most expensive. They tend to be booked by the same people for the same weeks year-after-year. However, thanks to the internet good fishing can often be booked by credit card at less than 24 hrs notice and often at remarkably low prices for good beats. This is often due to cancellations. Most Salmon rivers are linked to The Association of Salmon Fishery Boards *www.fisheries.asfb. org.uk* or *www.fishpal.com* others, like the Deveron, have their own web-based booking arrangements – see *www.deveron.org.*

How much does it cost?

Salmon fishing can cost from £5 a day to £2,000 a week per person. But many towns and villages on rivers have their own fishing and angling associations. They will usually sell day tickets for a few pounds. Hotels can often arrange fishing and may be able to loan equipment.

Can you sell a Salmon if you catch one?

No. It is illegal to sell a rod-caught Salmon or Sea trout in Scotland. This is to prevent poaching. You can eat it or give it away. Ironically the only genuinely wild Scottish Salmon that can be bought legally is one caught in nets in estuaries or along the coast. Netting is a controversial subject (see netting, p68).

Catch and release

Catch and release as a conservation measure is almost universal on Scottish rivers. Each river tends to have its own rules and guidelines for releasing Salmon and Sea trout. Most rivers allow a fisherman to keep one or two fish a week. Some have a total catch and release policy. Many rivers reward fishermen with a side of farmed smoked Salmon or a bottle of whisky for returning fish. But you will need proof! Some beats or rivers insist on the use of barbless hooks to reduce damage and trauma. Most rivers insist that all 'springers', salmon arriving in spring and early summer, must be returned ever since numbers started dropping. By the autumn fish of both sexes will be 'coloured' dark red (often referred to as 'kippers') indicating they are in spawning mode and ought to be released. As a conservation measure, most fishermen will anyway return the 'hen' or female fish which carry eggs. Fish that are damaged are normally kept – a decision left to the fisherman.

River bank etiquette

How to behave is largely common sense. A fisherman who arrives on the river bank when another is already fishing should start fishing upstream. On a river you should move a pace or two downstream before making the next cast. Fishing the same spot only frightens the fish and means others  cannot move down stream. The same common sense rules govern loch fishing from a boat: don't start fishing downwind of another boat already on the water. Canoeists and rafters generally have a right to be on the river but also a responsibility to cause least disturbance to anglers.

If asked to fish as a guest you should offer any fish you catch to your host – depending on local catch and release rules. If you are lucky they will insist you keep it. Some don't. It's their fish after all.

There is no need to engage a fisherman on the other bank in lengthy conversation because you usually cannot hear anything above the noise of the water. A wave and 'Any luck?' is quite sufficient.

Can you catch trout if you are fishing for Salmon – and vice versa?

If you have permission to fish for Salmon and Sea trout on a river you will usually be allowed to fish for Brown trout as well. But permission to fish for Brown trout does not normally give you the right to catch Salmon and Sea trout. If in doubt ask. In the past, Brown trout fishing was free in many places. If you happened to catch a salmon by mistake you had to put it back. The free Brown trout rule only applies in very few places today.

Who owns and regulates fishing?

Rivers and fishing are all owned by someone. It could be a farmer, a local town or county council, a large estate or an individual. It is not generally owned by the state/government. Fishing is regulated locally by 'salmon district boards' legal authorities composed of angling clubs, local councils, netsmen and 'riparian owners' – riverbank owners (from the Latin ripa, a bank). The laws governing salmon, once a major food source and commodity, are ancient and were introduced to prevent poaching. Most rivers are supported by separate charities or trusts which raise money to carry out river improvements and work closely with boards. They have their own Rivers and Fisheries Trusts of Scotland *www.rafts.org.uk*

When to catch fish

Fish will 'take', or bite, at almost any time of day. Early morning, noon and dusk seem to be best. Water conditions are important and each 'beat' or stretch has its own water heights when the chances of catching a fish are at their best. Ideally, the water height should be beginning to drop following rain. The fresh water brings the fish up river. The water should be fairly clear, not 'coloured'– black or red from peat or mud. The day should be overcast with a light downstream wind. Less favourable: bright sun, mist on the water

and a water temperature higher than the air temperature. Raw prawns and shrimps mounted on hooks are supposed to be deadly, so they are banned on most rivers. Prawns and shrimps are part of a salmon's diet at sea, although salmon do not feed in the river. So when fish spot a prawn they either go mad for it or turn tail and run.

Rods

Modern rods are made of carbon fibre and are half the weight of the old greenheart wood and cane rods used up to the 1960s when fibre glass became increasingly popular. Salmon rods tend to be around 14-15ft long. An all round rod for salmon and smaller sea trout can be about 10.6ins to 12ft. Trout rods vary from 8-9ft. Prices run from £20 to £400. Hardy, Sage, Greys and Sharpes are the big names in rod making. But Japanese-owned Daiwa which has a factory in Wishaw, in central Scotland, has a big following.

The Conflicts

Fish Farming

Since fish farms were introduced to sea lochs and river estuaries on the West Coast of Scotland, catches of wild Salmon and Sea trout have declined. Fishermen and river owners blame sea lice from fish farms. The lice escape from the cages and attach themselves to migrating wild fish. The lice literally eat the fish alive.

Lice have now become resistant to at least three generations of chemicals designed to control numbers in the cages.

In spite of all the evidence that sea lice are affecting stocks of wild fish (protected by EU legislation) the Scottish Government wants anglers and fish farmers to compromise. This is because there is no other industry in the West Highlands apart from local government, seasonal tourism and subsistence level agriculture. Fish farming is seen as an economic life line.

Netting

Salmon has been netted commercially on the coast and in estuaries probably for thousands of years. Although the number of operating netting stations has dwindled, anglers claim netsmen are damaging stocks of wild Salmon through non-selective netting. However, the Scottish Government has been backing netsmen with grants in an attempt to support the last of a traditional industry. Coastal nets are rigged at right angles to the shore. As the Salmon swims along the coast in search of its home river it runs into the nets. Only a net-caught Salmon can be legally sold as 'wild' Scotch Salmon. It is illegal to sell rod caught fish. The netting season varies around the coast generally runs from April 1 to August 30.

Salmon catches

Perhaps surprisingly the number of Salmon caught on rod and line has remained fairly consistent since official records began,

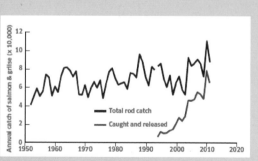

in spite of a reduction in coastal netting effort and increased angling effort. Catches are affected by climate, mortality at sea, fish farming and netting. In 2012, the total rod catch was 84,950 with 74 per cent released. The Sea trout total was 21,691.

Ways to Fish

Fishing with a fly

Most Salmon and Sea trout fishing is done with a fly that sinks below the surface, which is known for obvious reasons, as a 'wet' fly. Salmon are occasionally caught on a 'dry' fly which floats on the surface like an insect (deer hair, being hollow makes good dry fly material). Generally speaking, a fisherman will 'cast' or throw out the line at an angle of about 45 degrees. The fly will then be pulled down and across the river by the current. The fish tend to lie on the edge of the slack water and the main stream. Sea trout are caught in much the same way but often at night in midsummer. Brown trout in rivers tend to be at their best up until May and are usually caught on a wet fly. But a dry fly will do. Fishing from a boat on a loch, the fly is cast down wind and gradually pulled in, or dabbled on the surface.

Fishing with a spinner or lure

Not all rivers or owners allow spinning which traditionally was used in high water when a fly would not work. It can be more successful than fly fishing, probably because the lure sinks to the same level as the fish. (Flies tend to stay nearer the surface.) Fish caught on a treble-hooked spinner are often damaged and cannot be sensibly returned to the river. On a river the line is thrown out at right angles to the bank and reeled in.

Fishing with a worm

Fishing with a worm is far more difficult than it sounds and it is not allowed on most rivers. It is reserved normally for high water and 'spates'- major surges of water – when nothing else will work. A line weighted two foot from the hooked worm is 'trotted', or bounced, down the river bed in the hope of finding a fish hiding on the bottom. But it is conservation unfriendly. The fish usually swallows the whole worm and the hook cannot be extracted. It can work well with Brown trout in hill 'burns' or streams.

Fishing flies

'Flies catch more fishermen than fish,' it is said. Most fishermen have boxes full of colourful flies but use very few! The use of artificial flies as bait can be traced to ancient Macedonia. Most Salmon and Sea trout in Scotland are caught on a wet fly which sinks below the surface although both can be caught on dry flies. Flies made for the Spey are famous for their size and colour. The popular Ally's Shrimp and Cascade invented by Ally Gowans on the Tay are renowned for catching both Salmon and Sea trout.

Greenwells Glory is hard to beat for trout. Stocked trout in fisheries will take multicoloured flies tied in lurex. Local knowledge in all cases is invaluable.

Hair of the dog

Fishermen who tie their own flies usually get round to using the hair of their own dog. Christopher Burges-Lumsden of Aberdeenshire has tied flies with most breeds of dog including his late mother's Pekinese. 'The Peke is not a good swimmer. Any fly tied with Peke hair will go straight to the bottom.' But that's exactly what fishermen want in spring when the rivers are still high and the fish are deep down. 'Later on you want a bit of Collie,' he says. A fly tied with collie hair (pictured) will swim somewhere in the middle between the surface and the bottom. For days when the fish are nearer the surface Mr. Burges-Lumsden switches to black Labrador, a well known favourite among fly tiers and good for tying the Stoats Tail a classic sea trout fly. Many a fish has been caught by hair of the dog. Deer hair is sometimes used to make dry flies for salmon. The hair is hollow so it floats.

PETER KEYSER / www.peterkeyser.com

Salmon *Salmo salar*

To the serious fisherman 'a fish' is not any old fish. It is specifically a Salmon. Nothing else counts. 'We've had 10 fish this week' means, the party has caught 10 salmon even though they may have caught half a dozen sea trout and countless Brown trout besides. Most people of course are delighted to catch anything at all. Salmon are caught conventionally on a fly or spinner and less conventionally and often illegally, on a worm , shrimp or prawn.

Salmon have had a special place in the mind of man for thousands, possibly millions, of years. The Celts believed the fish was endowed with powers of wisdom. The Picts carved images of a Salmon in their standing stones, long before a fish became Christian symbol. (The Romans were amazed to find the Picts refused to eat salmon even though the rivers were teeming with fish). The salmon is indeed a rare fish. Almost magically it lives in both saltwater and freshwater and it returns to the same river year after year.

Life cycle of a Salmon

An 11lb (5kg) female will lay about 8,000 eggs of which perhaps 10 will actually survive to became adult salmon. They lay them in the late autumn in small shallow burns at the top of the rivers in gravel areas known as redds.

About 400 will survive to become 'fingerlings'. After a year they are called 'parr' and stay in the river for 2-4 years before they become 'smolts'. Smolts go to sea for up to four years and return to the same river where they hatched. Fish that spend only one year at sea before returning to their original river are called 'grilse' and will weigh around 5lb.

How do Salmon manage to find their home river?

They probably navigate across the ocean using the earth's electromagnetic fields, the sun and the stars. Once they have arrived on the coast they find their own river by following the shore line until they pick up the chemical marker unique to their river. Smell may be involved too. In the river, another chemical marker will guide them to their home burn, or stream, and native spawning ground or 'redds'. Salmon do not feed once they have returned to their home river. So it's a mystery why they will snatch at an artificial fly or lure. When they first arrive in a river snatching at a bait is probably a reflex action left over from feeding at sea. Consequently, 'beats' – stretches of river – near a river mouth tend to be the most productive. But as fish move further upstream away from the sea snatching at a fly is more likely to be an aggressive reaction. The longer they stay in the river the darker they become. Sea lice on the skin indicate the fish is fresh from the sea.

BOB WHITE, STANLEY

Playing a good Salmon caught fly fishing from the boat in Horsey on the Pitlochrie beat at Stanley, Perthshire, Scotland.

Brown trout *Salmo trutta*

Brown trout are the wild native fish of Britain and northern Europe. They are found in almost every river, loch and burn in Scotland. They can weigh more than 30lbs (13.6kg) and live for over 20 years. A 2lb (0.9kg) wild 'brownie' in Scotland is considered a good catch. Size depends largely on the quality and quantity of food available. They eat insects of all sorts unless they go carnivorous (see Ferox, below) Each female produces about 2,000 eggs of which only around 20 per cent survive to adulthood. Brown trout are also reared for 'put and take' trout fisheries. They can be caught on a fly, spinner or worm.

Ferox trout *Salmo ferox*

Ferox are Brown trout that switch from eating invertebrates to eating other fish – usually Arctic Char, a land-locked hangover from the Ice Age found mainly in large and deep Highland lochs. Ferox will also eat Brown trout and are often referred to as cannibals. The diet of fresh meat turns them into monsters and Ferox hold all the trout records. The biggest have come from Loch Awe in Argyllshire weighing more than 30lbs. Ferox are fished from a boat and can be successfully caught on a weighted lure near the bottom. Ferox fishing tends to be for Ferox enthusiasts, but has become increasingly popular.

Brown trout: the wild, native fish of Britain

CACTUS.MAN

Loch Leven trout

Trout eggs from Loch Leven have been shipped all over the world since the mid 19th century, usually to improve fishing for British colonists. In 1899 The Duke of Bedford sent 10,000 Loch Leven trout eggs to the Maharaja of Kashmir which perished *en route.* The next consignment fared better and were reared by a keen British angler Frank J Mitchell in his carpet factory in Srinagar. To this day the snowy waters of the Kashmiri rivers bubble with brown trout whose ancestors were born in Kinross.

Loch Leven trout which can grow to 9lbs (4.1kg) have been shipped to Argentina, the Falkland Islands, Australia and New Zealand.

Sea trout *Salmo trutta morpha trutta*

Sea trout have a reputation as tremendous fighting fish. Surprisingly, they are the same species as Brown trout. A Sea trout is simply a Brown trout that migrates to the sea at 2-3 years and changes colour from brown to silver. Most Sea trout are females in search of a richer food source to build up their energy for spawning. The males laze about in the river. Sea trout tend to stay close to the coast before returning each year to spawn. In the sea they feed on sand eels and sprats and are generally larger than Brown trout as a result of their diet. But they share the same 'redds' or spawning beds as Brown trout. In Scotland, Sea trout grow to about 5lbs (2.2kg) although the record is 22lbs (10kg) caught in 1989 in the River Leven that flows out of Loch Lomond. Generally, 3lbs (1.3kg) is considered a good size. Juvenile Sea trout returning for the first time are known as finnock, herling or sewin in different parts of Scotland. Sea trout tend to appear in Scottish lochs, rivers and estuaries around June. They can be caught at any time of day but are most active at night. Fishing for Sea trout in midsummer when it scarcely gets dark in the north of Scotland, Orkney and Shetland is a fisherman's dream. Sea trout can be caught on a fly in salt water sea lochs and river estuaries on a rising tide. A predominantly black Stoat's Tail fly, is probably the classic Sea trout fly.

 **Rainbow trout** (*Oncorhynchus mykiss*) is a Pacific salmonid species that was first brought to Britain in 1884. Fast-growing and tolerant of crowding in captivity, they are now widely used around the world for fish farming and restocking trout fisheries. If they escape from ponds or hatcheries they seldom breed in the wild, and will eat Salmon eggs.

Coarse fishing

Scotland has some of Europe's best coarse fishing. But game fishing – trout and salmon – tends to take precedence. There is no closed season for coarse fishing in Scotland. It is illegal to use live bait. Fishing may be free but you must ask permission.

Pike *Esox lucius*
Scotland holds the UK record for Pike – 47lbs on Loch Lomond. But they can grow up to 70lbs. They are predators and feed on other fish and ducklings.Where smaller fish feed – so do Pike! They are caught either with a bait suspended from a float or weighted near the bottom.

Arctic Char *Salvelinus alpinus*
Closely related to salmon and trout, char can grow to 3lbs-4lbs in deep glacial Highland lochs such as Awe and Arkaig. They can live at a depth of 100-200ft and are caught from a boat with spinner or sometimes maggots and at night on a fly when they come to the surface.

Grayling *Thymallus thymallus*
An underestimated imported member of the salmon family from 1lb -3lb found in many rivers south of Perthshire, notably Tweed. They can be caught in the winter on a fly, worm or spinner. Grayling swim in shoals and taste of thyme – hence the name.
www.wheretofish.spinfish.co.uk

The Female Touch

Intriguingly most of the records for catching large salmon are held by women.

One of the theories advanced to explain women's extraordinary success at catching salmon is that the fish are attracted by female pheremones – essentially a chemical sex appeal. As the biggest Salmon are male or 'cock' fish it is said they are attracted to a fly or line handled by a woman. Salmon have a very powerful sense of smell. It may be one of the ways they find their way home to spawn.

Men, on the other hand, appear to have a negative effect on fish. There have been stories of men putting one finger into a river and stopping a salmon ascending a fish ladder – seen through an observation window. When a woman put her hand in, the fish were undeterred.

But there may be a less exotic explanation as to why women are successful anglers. Princess Diana's mother, the late Frances Shand-Kydd was a noted and successful Spey fisherwoman. 'I move like a panther in the water. And I think most women are just less clumsy than men. Added to that they get on with the job of fishing, unlike men who spend a lot of time drinking and gossiping in the fishing hut.'

Others say that women are prepared to listen to advice from ghillies and follow it, unlike men who can think they know it all.

The British record for salmon is still held by Georgina Ballantine, a ghillie's daughter who landed a 64-pounder fishing on the Tay at Glendelvine in October 1922. Georgina however was using a baited lure.

The record for the largest fish caught on a fly goes to Mrs. 'Tiny' Morison (right), fishing the Deveron in October 1924. Her fish weighed 61lbs. It was caught on a little known fly, a Brown Winged Killer, at Mountblairy, Banffshire. The fish was too big for the estate scales so it had to be taken the next day to the nearest railway station which in those days had scales on the platform.

What to wear

On the river pretty well anything goes as long as you can stay warm and dry. You are likely to need anything from a Souwester for the rain to a baseball cap for the sun. Small auto-inflatable life jackets are increasingly advised. Fishing has never quite acquired the formality that can be encountered on some shoots. Anyway, waders and skirts don't go together. Basking in the sun beside a Scottish river with a picnic is as good as it gets.

Salmon Rivers and their Seasons

All dates inclusive but liable to change

Ailort		Feb 11 – Oct 31	Earn			Feb 1 – Oct 31
Aline		Feb 11 – Oct 31	Eden	*Fife*		Feb 15 – Oct 31
Almond		Jan 15 – Oct 15	Esk	*Border*		Feb 1 – Oct 31
Alness		Feb 11 – Oct 31	Etive			Feb 11 – Oct 15
Amhuinnsuidhe *Isle of Harris*		Jun 15 – Oct 15	Etterick			Feb 1 – Nov 30
Annan		Feb 25 – Nov 15	Evelix			Jan 11 – Sep 30
Arnisdale		Feb 11 – Oct 31	Ewe			Feb 11 – Oct 31
Aros	*Isle of Mull*	Feb 11 – Oct 31	Fincastle – Borve Fishings			
Awe		Feb 11 – Oct 15			*Isle of Harris*	Feb 25 – Oct 31
Ba	*Isle of Mull*	Feb 11 – Oct 31	Findhorn			Feb 11 – Sep 30
Beauly		Feb 11 – Oct 15	Fhorsa *Uig Lodge - Isle of Lewis*			
Berriedale		Feb 11 – Oct 31				Jun 1 – Oct 15
Bladnoch		Feb 11 – Oct 31	Fleet	*Kirkcudbright*		Feb 25 – Oct 31
Blackwater *Isle of Lewis*		Feb 25 – Oct 15	Fleet	*Sutherland*		Feb 25 – Oct 31
Borgie		Jan 12 – Sep 30	Forss			Feb 11 – Oct 31
Broom		Feb 11 – Oct 31	Forth			Feb 1 – Oct 31
Brora		Feb 1 – Oct 15	Garry			Jan 15 – Oct 15
Carron	*West Coast*	Feb 11 – Oct 31	Gour			Feb 11 – Oct 31
Carron *Kyle of Sutherland*		Jan 11 – Sep 30	Girvan			Feb 25 – Oct 31
Cassley		Jan 11 – Sep 30	Gress	*Isle of Lewis*		Jun 1 – Oct 15
Clyde		Feb 11 – Oct 31	Grimersta	*Isle of Lewis*		Jun 3 – Oct 15
Conon		Feb 11 – Sep 30	Grudie			Feb 11 – Oct 31
Cree		Mar 1 – Oct 14	Gruinard & Little Gruinard			Feb 11 – Oct 31
Creed	*Isle of Lewis*	Jun 1 – Oct 15	Halladale			Jan 12 – Sep 30
Dee	*Aberdeenshire*	Feb 1 – Sep 30	Helmsdale			Jan 11 – Sep 30
Dee	*Kirkcudbright*	Feb 11 – Oct 31	Hamanavay *Isle of Lewis*			Jun 1 – Oct 15
Deveron		Feb 11 – Oct 31	Hope & Loch Hope			Jan 12 – Sep 30
Dionard		Feb 11 – Oct 31	Inver			Feb 11 – Oct 31
Don		Feb 11 – Oct 31	Iorsa	*Isle of Arran*		Feb 25 – Oct 31
Doon		Feb 11 – Oct 31	Irvine			Feb 25 – Nov 15
Dunbeath		Feb 11 – Oct 15	Isla			Jan 15 – Oct 15
Dundonnell		Feb 11 – Oct 31	Kannaird			Feb 11 – Oct 31
Eachaig		May 1 – Oct 31	Kirkaig			Feb 11 – Oct 31

**Toasting
the Deveron
on the opening
day of the season**

Kishorn		Feb 11 – Oct 31
Laggan	*Isle of Islay*	Feb 25 – Oct 31
Laxadale Fishings *Isle of Harris*		
		Apr 1 – Oct 15
Laxford		Feb 11 – Oct 31
Laxay Fishery	*Isle of Lewis*	Feb 25 – Oct 31
Leven	*Dumbartonshire*	Feb 11 – Oct 31
Lochy		Feb 11 – Oct 31
Lossie		Feb 25 – Oct 31
Luce		Feb 25 – Oct 31
Lussa	*Isle of Mull*	Feb 11 – Oct 31
Machrie	*Isle of Arran*	Feb 25 – Oct 31
Moidart		Feb 11 – Oct 31
Morar		Feb 11 – Oct 31
Nairn		Feb 11 – Oct 7
Naver		Jan 12 – Sep 30
Ness		Jan 15 – Oct 15
Nith		Feb 25 – Nov 30
North Esk		Feb 16 – Oct 31
Obbe System *Isle of Harris*		Jun 15 – Oct 31
Orkney Islands Fishings		Feb 25 – Oct 31
Orchy		Feb 11 – Oct 15
Oykel		Jan 11 – Sep 30
Polla		Jan 12 – Sep 30
Polly		Feb 11 – Oct 15
Rhiconich		Feb 11 – Oct 15
Rodel Fishings *Isle of Harris*		Mar 1 – Sep 30

Ruel		Feb 16 – Oct 31
Sanda		Feb 11 – Oct 31
Scaddie		Feb 11 – Oct 31
Shetland Islands Fishings		Feb 25 – Oct 31
Shiel and Loch Shiel		Feb 11 – Oct 31
Shin		Jan 11 – Sep 30
Sligachan	*Isle of Skye*	Feb 11 – Oct 15
Snizort	*Isle of Skye*	Feb 11 – Oct 15
Sorn	*Isle of Islay*	Feb 25 – Oct 31
South Esk		Feb 16 – Oct 31
Spey		Feb 11 – Sep 30
Stinchar		Feb 25 – Oct 31
Strathy		Jan 12 – Sep 30
Tay		Jan 15 – Oct 15
Teviot		Feb 1 – Nov 30
Thurso		Jan 11 – Oct 5
Till		Feb 1 – Nov 30
Torridon		Feb 11 – Oct 31
Tummel		Jan 15 – Oct 15
Tweed		Feb 1 – Nov 30
Ugie		Feb 10 – Oct 31
Ullapool		Feb 11 – Oct 31
Urr		Feb 25 – Nov 30
Whiteadder & Blackadder		Feb 1 – Nov 30
Wick		Feb 11 – Oct 31
Yarrow Water		Feb 1 – Nov 30
Ythan		Feb 11 – Oct 31

Stalking

Stalking is perhaps the purest of all field sports, pitting man's cunning against the razor sharp instincts of a wild animal. Not only is stalking humane, it is selective and requires skill. Monarch of the Glen, the famous painting of a stag by Sir Edwin Landseer, Queen Victoria's favourite artist, sums up for many the majesty and romanticism of the Highlands.

Successfully stalking a Red deer stag across rugged, treeless hillsides in all weathers can be one of life's most exhilarating sporting experiences. Nonetheless, the art of stalking woodland Roe deer is also hugely popular, excellent value and particularly popular with visitors from Germany, Belgium and Italy.

Deer are ruminants and digest their food in two stages. They are cloven-hoofed with an even number of toes, like goats, cattle and sheep. They feed on grasses, heather, berries, lichens and mosses. They will also eat tree seedlings and the bark of trees.

Which species of deer can be stalked?

Red deer (*Monarch of the Glen*) and Roe. Sika and Fallow are also present in some parts of Scotland. Only Red deer and Roe are native to the UK. All the others were introduced.

Deer management

Deer are wild animals which can cause serious damage to agricultural crops and particularly woodland. Deer management in Scotland is designed to maintain a healthy balance between the demands of animal welfare and the interests of agriculture, forestry and sport. Too many deer can lead to overgrazing, shortage of food and starvation in winter. Too few can alter the natural balance in the hills, deprive landowners of sporting and venison income and reduce employment opportunities.

Deer roam freely and do not recognise man-made boundaries. Scotland is now split up into about 70 voluntary deer management groups, mainly in the uplands, made up of sporting, forestry and environmental interests. Annual deer counts are organised by each group which sets a figure for the cull in consultation with Scottish Natural Heritage, the body which has overall responsibility for Scotland's flora and fauna.

Rifles

Rifles are used for deer stalking and pest control, particularly foxes. Modern rifles and ammunition are extremely accurate. With a good telescopic sight it is possible to drop a big stag stone dead at 200yds (183m) or more, although the stalker's skill is to get as close as possible. In Scotland, the type of single shot sporting rifle that can be used is set out in law which stipulates the minimum calibre, velocity and energy that may be used.

- The .308 is the largest calibre in general use for stalking Red deer.
- The .270 is a popular all rounder capable of dealing with stags and hinds of all sizes.
- The .243 is similarly popular and about the smallest calibre for on Red or Fallow deer.
- The .22 'centre-fire', ie .222, is the minimum size than can be used for Roe deer.
- The .22 'rim-fire' is a standard size for rabbits and all pests.
- The .17 is a fantastically accurate long range calibre for pest control with a tiny bullet, but affected by wind.

The technical stuff

In Scotland, all deer may be shot with a minimum 100 grain bullet travelling at 2,450 Feet Per Second (FPS) giving 1,750 Foot Pound Energy (FPE). Roe may be shot with a minimum 50 grain bullet travelling at least 2,450 FPS to give 1,000 FPE. The 'expanding', hollow or soft nose bullet must be used by law to maximise stopping power.

LINDA MELLOR

Who makes the best rifles?

All a matter of opinion. First rate mass produced rifles include Sako, Tikka, Ruger and Mannlicher at less than £1,000. A bespoke custom-made rifle from Holland & Holland will cost around £30,000. Smaller but equally good makers include Precison Rifle Services of Tomintoul who will charge around £7,000. The classic John Rigby .275, a useable collectors item, is hard to beat. Telescopic sites can cost from £500-£5,000. A bipod and sound moderator (silencer) may cost another £500.

Deer

Red deer *Cervus elaphus*

Red deer are Britain's largest native wild mammals with no significant predators since the disappearance of wolves, although an eagle will take a calf and so will a fox. Although deer are woodland animals Red deer have uniquely adapted over hundreds of years to live on open hillsides in the Highlands. Scottish hill stags tend to  be smaller than their woodland dwelling cousins and generally weigh, when mature, between 12 and 20 stone (70kg-127kg). The hinds will be nine to 11 stone (57-70kg). In Scotland, stags average around 80inches (201cms) in head and body and up to 50inches (126cms) high at the shoulder and females average 71inches (180cm) long and 45inches (114cms) tall. Stags are shot between July 1 and October 20. Hinds, which are more numerous, can be shot from October 21 to February 15.

Stags and hinds live in separate sex groups. During the autumn mating season, known as 'the rut', mature stags compete for the hinds. Rival stags challenge opponents by roaring and grunting and walking in parallel to size each other up. If neither backs down they will clash antlers. The winner mates with a 'harem' or group of up to, perhaps, 40 hinds. Hinds commonly give birth at the beginning of their third summer after a gestation period of 240-260 days. Fawns, which can stand within a few hours of birth, lose their spots by the end of the summer and remain with their mother for up to a year. Hinds bark when alarmed and moo when looking for a calf.

Red deer generally live for 10-13 years in the wild and up to 20 years in captivity. Red deer meat, like all venison, is almost fat free and better served slightly red. The liver is deliciously tender, but not to everyone's taste.

Roe deer *Capreolus capreolus*

In Scotland it is estimated there is probably one Roe deer per square kilometre – to the point they are often considered to be pests. Roe are enchanting animals, but can cause serious damage to trees and crops and are increasingly involved in road accidents. Roe, which live as small territorial family groups, are woodland animals. They are most easily spotted at dawn and dusk feeding on the edge of stubble fields or woodland clearings. They are now seen in semi urban parks and on golf courses, and even on the open hill along with Red deer. Roe can produce one or two 'kids' in May/June. Bucks have a pair of single spiky antlers up to 9inches (22.9cm) long. The meat is often as tender as prime lamb.

Sika *Cervus nippon*

Originally from Asia and introduced in the 19th century as an ornamental species which, needless to say, escaped. They are smaller and more compact than Red deer. They are now well established in around 40 per cent of the Red deer range and will interbreed.

Fallow deer *Dama dama*

Introduced to England in the 11th or 12th century for hunting, fallow are found in relatively isolated pockets in those areas where they were originally kept in enclosures for meat. There have been large herds around Dunkeld, Perthshire and in a number of other places across Scotland. The place name 'Deer park' often indicates an old enclosure.

How many deer are there in Scotland?

Precise numbers are hard to estimate. Deer are, after all, wild animals. The best estimate is that there are up to 800,000 in total comprising 300,000 Red deer, up to 400,000 Roe and 100,000 other species.

What is culling?

Culling is the selection and shooting of weaker older or injured animals. 'Stalking' is the term often used for the culling operation, a necessary part of deer management. The majority of animals culled each year are the more numerous female 'hinds'. Stalking is often let and the income helps cover the costs of deer management.

> **Cull** *(verb) pick out, select. First recorded in c13th as culen, to choose, select; and earlier as cullen, to put through a strainer. From Old French and earlier Latin colliegere – collect.*

How many deer are culled each year?

It varies depending on the size of the herds. In 2011-12 about 85,000 Red and Roe deer were culled but the number will vary annually. Deer are successful breeders and survivors, so the numbers will vary each year.

Did you know:

- Deer are thought to be colour blind - to some colours.
- Deer pick up movement but very little detail.
- On a windless day, deer can hear over 400 yards.
- Deer can rotate their ears in any direction.
- Deer's sense of smell is 20 times better than humans.

Trees, crops and deer

Deer can cause substantial economic damage through grazing young tree shoots and agricultural crops. But to remove them completely from an area could alter the natural balance in the landscape and lead to job losses among stalkers and reduced income from sport and venison. Like most ecological problems the solutions are often unclear, changeable and passionately argued. But the Red deer is a survivor.

Hill walking and deer

The 'Heading for the Scottish Hills' website alerts walkers to deer stalking activity so they can plan alternative routes. But it does not cover all areas. Walkers have a right of responsible access to the hills but are advised to keep to known paths which deer will avoid anyway. Deer are easily spooked. The website relies on stalking parties keeping it up to date. Stalkers also have to be aware walkers can appear without warning. *www.outdoor-scotland.com*.

Wild Goats

Feral Goats are found in pockets all the way up the west of Scotland from Galloway to Cape Wrath and even Speyside. They are probably the descendents of goats abandoned by crofters during the land Clearances of the c18th. The male 'billies' are shot for their spectacular horned heads. A number of websites offer goat stalking.

MELANIE/ lastinglight.co.uk

Who can go stalking?

Anyone provided they have permission from the landowner and are legally entitled to carry a firearm.

How do you find out about stalking?

There are numerous websites offering stalking of all sorts at all prices throughout Scotland – particularly Roe deer stalking. The Scottish Country Sports Tourism Group (*www.countrysportscotland.com*) is a good place to start. CKDGalbraith is one of the largest sporting agents in Scotland.

Other useful sites:

The British Deer Society *www.bds.org.uk*
BASC *www.basc.org.uk* for rifle information
Association of Deer Management Groups *www.deer-management.co.uk*

Who owns the stalking?

Sporting rights usually go with land. Whoever has the sporting rights owns the stalking.

Antlers

Red deer 'cast' or shed antlers at the end of winter. Growing antlers are covered with 'velvet', a soft, blood-filled, bone-forming tissue which is very sensitive. Red deer will have lost the velvet by September in time for the 'rut' (mating season). Cast antlers are a food source for small mammals and birds that are in turn food for larger predators like birds of prey and foxes – all part of the natural food chain. They are also chewed by deer themselves as source of calcium.

How many points does a deer have on its antlers?

It depends entirely on age and the condition of the animal and its habitat. In general, the better fed the stag the greater the number of points, and the heavier the antlers.

A Red deer with 12 points (six per antler) is known as a Royal. A 14-pointer is an Imperial and a 16-pointer a Monarch. The stag in the Landseer painting is a Royal not a Monarch. In the world of Roe buck stalking there is considerable demand for 'medal' heads, as good quality heads are known. Mature Roe antlers will be up to 30cm long with three tines or points on each antler. Sika antlers are not as wide as Red deer and are anyway smaller if similar. All deer antlers can be graded by CIC the international organisation that sets the standard. Scotland has its own CIC graders. *www.cictrophy.com*

Can I sell a deer if I shoot one?

Licensed estates can sell venison direct to the public 'at the farm gate' or through a venison dealer. The carcass is usually kept and sold by the estate or stalker as part of their income. Arrangements to keep a carcass can be made.

How much does venison sell for?

In 2012 estates could expect anything from £2.50 per kilo for the carcase. The price in the supermarket or restaurant will be considerably more . Farm and estate shops such as Finzean on Royal Deeside (*www.finzean.com*) offer special deals on venison cuts. Venison is becoming increasingly popular and

Driving Tip

Deer, particularly Roe, tend to cross the road at night singly or in small family groups. If you brake for one, keep braking. A second and even a third will almost certainly cross just when you thought you'd missed the first. If you do hit one you cannot claim against the landowner as they are wild animals. Theoretically you cannot take the carcass. It belongs to the roads' authority or the owner of the land where it lies.

is no more expensive than many other meats. It is also virtually fat-free and can be turned into everything from mince to burgers and sausages. Cooking methods are similar to beef and lamb but with so little natural fat most cooks will marinade the meat overnight and rub in oil or butter.

How much does stalking cost?

Costs depend a great deal on where and what you are stalking: generally the better the stags or more prestigious the estate, the more it will cost. A day's stalking for a Red deer stag in 2012 cost anything from £240–£600. At the basic level that included a trained stalker/keeper with a 4x4 and use of a rifle. Hinds were between £50 and £360 and Sika stags £250–£300. Roe buck stalking can start from £40 unaccompanied rising to £150 an outing with a keeper. A Fallow buck will be £200 upwards. 'Trophy' fees for a good head are conditional and can be considerable.

Tipping a stalker for his efforts is traditional and up to the guest, starting in 2012 at around £30–£40 for a day.

Stalking: What Happens?

Red deer

A stalker will usually take guests out on a range for a few practice shots on a paper target or steel cut out silhouette of a stag. Estates usually provide rifles free of charge and often prefer guests to use their rifles because they know they are accurate and safe.

The stalker will take a guest out to an area where he has either spied deer recently or knows from experience where they will be in certain weather conditions. The trip out is likely to be by 4x4. Some estates insist on the traditional 'long walk in'.

Having spied a suitable beast, which may take several hours of driving and walking, the stalker will use the lie of the land for cover to work upwind of the quarry. His biggest fear is spooking other deer which will in turn spook his target. The guest will follow close behind. When in position the stalker will pull the rifle from its cover and beckon the guest to crawl forward and take the shot. Ideally the animal will be sideways on to present a clear view

of the heart area at a range of 100-200 metres or a little more. Deer are not shot on the move except in extreme circumstances. The 'gralloch' or innards are left on the hill for carrion. Stalker (or 'ghillie') and guest will have been followed at some distance by the 'pony boy', frequently a trainee, with a Highland Pony known as a 'garron'. He may use a tracked vehicle or 'Argo' to pick up the carcase, as a trophy of the day, and take it back to the game larder. Estates may prepare the antlers for a guest to take away.

The deer pizzle or penis of a stag is highly prized in Far East medicine as an aphrodisiac.

Red deer hinds

Hind stalking tends to be for the serious enthusiast. Large numbers of hinds have to be culled each year. The cull is generally carried out by estate stalkers who have to work quickly and efficiently often between bad weather during the winter. Not all estates will take out guests during the cull.

Roe deer

Roe can be stalked on foot through woodland or ambushed as they graze. Some farmers and landowners are happy to let experienced shots go out by themselves. Quite often, a bottle of whisky or a reasonable cash payment is all a farmer will want. The stalker will have to move very quietly through the landscape. Roe are spooked by the slightest noise or movement, or change in the wind, and can be difficult to see. Supporting sticks can be used for standing shots. Alternatively, there is the 'high seat', a free standing scaffold or wooden structure with a clear view of a known Roe grazing area or route. Portable high seats can be propped up against trees. The marksman often needs to be in position before dawn or late afternoon.

Are deer reared specially for stalking?

Very seldomly. But there may be a few stags that are fed and reserved for their size.

Why is a deer forest called a forest when there are no trees?

A forest does not always mean trees. The word comes from the Latin *foris*, meaning waste or open, in other words hunting land. The Caledonian Forest which covered huge areas of Scotland was not a forest in the modern sense but untamed scrub and trees. Caledonia was the Romans' name for Scotland, from the early Celtic caleto, meaning 'hard, strong'.

Where to see Red deer

While Red deer are resident all year round, they tend to spend the summer up in the hills and remote glens, and only move down to lower levels in the winter, where food is more readily available. Population hotspots include Galloway Forest Park, the islands of Rum and Jura, Perthshire and the Northwest Highlands. Deer can often be seen through binoculars from the main A9 Perth-Inverness road, or even at the roadside itself. Glencoe, Glenshee and Drumochter are all likely spotting places.

They can also be seen at the following:
Beecraigs Country Park nr Linlithgow, West Lothian EH496PL
www.beecraigs.com t 01506 844516/844517/844518.

Glengoulandie Deer Park Keltneyburn, Aberfeldy, PH16 5NL
www.glengoulandie.co.uk t 01887 830495

The Highland Wildlife Park Kincraig
www.highlandwildlifepark.org t 01540 651270

Jedforest Deer and Farm Park Mervinslaw Estate, Jedburgh TD8 6PL
www.jedforestdeerpark.co.uk t 01835 840364.

The Scottish Deer Centre Cupar, Fife KY15 4NQ
www.tsdc.co.uk t 01337 810391

The Female Touch

Women take easily to stalking, particularly Red deer in the hills. Like fishing, stalking requires a willingness on the part of the guest to listen to the stalker/ghillie. But they need to be fit for a day of considerable exertion. There is also a practical side to stalking. Stags and hinds need to be culled to ensure the overall health of the herd.

Stalking requires not brute force and big bangs but stamina and finesse. There is the added attraction, for some, of being out alone in the heather with a stalker in rough tweeds and sinews of iron! And there are plenty of instances of so called 'well-born' women falling for gamekeepers, usually with disastrous consequences all round.

Women and men can often find shooting a stag an emotional experience. Not only is he male but he is big, wild and, there is no other word for it – noble. Women are equally adept in the woods, moving quietly through undergrowth in search of ultra sensitive Roe and Sika.

Hunting

In spite of being banned in Scotland in 2002 – two years earlier than England – fox hunting, or rather 'riding to hounds' is more popular than ever. Most pre-ban hunts still keep their packs of hounds, meet regularly in winter and are still in the fox control business. Instead of chasing a fox they are allowed to drive them towards waiting marksmen with shotguns or rifles.

Most registered packs in Scotland are in the Borders area with its strong tradition of hunting over rolling open hill and farmland.

Besides the mounted hunts there are four foot packs – the huntsmen are generally on foot, not horses – which are essentially fox control packs. They operate in hilly or enclosed country where mounted hunts would be useless. Gamekeepers and farmers call them in to clear foxes. Like the mounted hunts they only drive the fox towards marksmen. Hounds can chase the fox until it is 'flushed' when hounds should be stopped as soon as practical.

Hunts meet regularly through the season but tend not to advertise their 'meets' to avoid attracting hunt saboteurs. You need to make contact via websites for meet details. Following hunts on foot or by car is a long established tradition for enthusiasts. Most hunts hold a traditional Boxing Day meet, open to everyone, which is a social occasion to admire the horses and hounds. Joining a hunt or riding with a hunt as a visitor will usually require local contacts. The hunting season: November 1–March 1. The Master of Fox Hounds Association holds details of all registered hunts, their contacts and websites. *www.mfha.org.uk*. Most hunts have their own website.

Border Hunt
Duke of Buccleuch's Hunt
Dumfriesshire & Stewartry Hunt
Fife Foxhounds
Jed Forest Hunt

Kincardineshire Hunt
Lauderdale Hunt
Lanarkshire & Renfrewshire Hunt
Liddesdale Hunt
Strathappin Hunt

Eating and Drinking

Lunch, picnics and drink

A shooting lunch is a lunch like no other. It may be a quick sandwich and a flask of tea in the 4x4 on a walking day, or it can be three courses with pre-lunch gin and tonic and wine in a shoot 'bothy' in front of a roaring fire.

It can be 'piece' or sandwich in a 'piece bag' with an apple, a bar of chocolate and Thermos of soup to take on a day's stalking. Or it can be a sit down meal with champagne and lobsters in a grouse moor lunch hut. It can be a barbecue on the riverbank with a bottle of wine or beer cooling in the water. If you've been outside in all weathers the chances are, you have earned it.

Julia Drysdale, author of the original *Game Cookery Book* maintained a sit-down shooting lunch had to be kept simple so that everyone (the British in particular) could talk without thinking too hard about what they were eating. In winter any good but thick stew – beef, game, mutton or chicken – is always appreciated. Shepherds pies, moussaka and lasagne rarely get complaints. A pheasant shoot lunch in winter has to be eaten with certain briskness as darkness falls early and the birds start roosting.

The lunch venue depends a bit on the day. If it's a walking day with a couple of friends and dogs, the chances are everyone will bring sandwiches and Thermos and someone may bring beer or wine. Lunch could be in a farm building or barn set up with a table and chairs or simply out of the back of a vehicle. Alternatively, a bar lunch in a pub which allows you leave muddy boots at the door is ideal.

Driven shoot lunches tend to be smarter, with lunch and drink laid on by the host or owner. There will usually be plenty of wine, a stew with mashed potato and vegetables followed by cheese, perhaps a Stilton, coffee and sloe gin. Homemade orange gin is popular.

Grouse moor picnics, like a stalking lunch, need be no more than a sandwich, a flask of tea, chocolate biscuits, fruit and water from the burn although wine usually finds its way up the hill.

However, as grouse and grouse shooting are so special it is not unusual to make a special effort if only to celebrate the occasion. And after all it's meant to be fun. If there is a lunch hut – big estates can have several – or a favoured picnic spot, lunch will be brought up the hill in hampers by 4x4, usually by the hostess or lodge cook who will have had to organise everything. Expect any, or all, of the following: barbecued venison fillet, homemade patés and terrine, smoked salmon, quiches, hams, chicken and cold grouse, lobsters, wine and champagne.

Many sporting lodges and hotels will make up sandwiches or rolls packed in small haversacks which are laid out for guests to pick up in the morning.

'Elevenses'

'Elevenses' at around 11am(!) is a traditional midmorning break for any shooting party whether it is a walking day or a driven bird day. A day out is not simply about sport but meeting and talking. The shoot captain or host will bring a wicker basket of drink and snacks usually after the second drive of the morning. On a walking day it's probably a question of bringing out the hip flasks.

Elevenses may include Bullshot, consommé spiced up with vodka or sherry, or a nip of sloe gin or ginger wine. If you are lucky there may be hot mini sausage or pork pie. If you are on a driven grouse day – it's champagne time! Sometimes Elevenses can become lunch in winter. Some shoots prefer

to dispense with a full lunch and instead have a brief break, with sandwiches in the late forenoon and then carry on. It's known as 'shooting through'.

Fishing lunches

It depends whether you are out for a few casts by yourself or fishing with a party who have rented fishing with a hut on the bank.

On some rivers, notably the Spey and Tweed, fishing huts can be fully equipped mini chalets with fridges, stoves, tables and chairs and a barbecue – although quite possibly no mobile reception, which can be no bad thing.

Filleted salmon or sea trout fresh from the river, rolled in oatmeal and lightly barbecued on both sides, is hard to beat. As with shooting you can make as much or as little of lunch by the river as you like a modest picnic or a banquet.

What to put in a hip flask

What you put in a hip flask is a matter of taste. Sloe gin is a favourite; neat whisky (unless it has water added) can be an acquired taste; Rusty Nail, a mixture of whisky and Drambuie comes highly recommended.

Recipes

Everyone has their favourite way of cooking game, but these are the classics.

Roast Grouse

Older grouse can be hung for 2-4 days in an airy fly-free place to tenderise the flesh and bring out the flavour in cooking. Young grouse seldom need hanging. There are a great many grouse recipes. Grouse can be stewed, barbecued and even fried. But roast grouse is a classic. Prepare bird; insert seasoned butter, cover breasts with bacon and place on well buttered bread in a roasting tin. Roast at 190°C (375°F) for 35-40 mins. Remove bacon 10 mins beforehand to brown. Serve with bread sauce, fried breadcrumbs and gravy, green salad and crisps.

For barbecue or grilling, split open and force apart keeping flat with a skewer. Rub in seasoned butter and plenty of pepper and salt and juniper berries if you have them. Cook for around 15 mins.

Roast venison

Venison is virtually fat free which makes it the healthy option, but large joints need larding and rubbing with butter before roasting. A roast needs less cooking than you think as it keeps on cooking when out of the oven. Don't worry if the first slices look bloody. A leg or haunch of Roe deer is generally a better bet than Red deer. There is not as much of it but it is incredibly tender. All venison can do with marinating overnight although Roe is tender enough. Marinate in wine, brandy, olive oil onion, pepper and herbs. Venison also stews well and always benefits from the addition of two or three juniper berries, redcurrant or rowan jelly and wine. Roe and Red deer about 15 mins per lb (0.5kg) for large joints (more than 4lbs (1.6kg) and 20mins per 1lb for smaller. Baste every 10 mins. A whole red deer can hang for 1-3 weeks in a well-aired larder before its ready to eat.

Pheasant

By the end of the season most keepers will sell you pheasant for 25p each, if you are lucky enough to have the contacts. Pluck and roast like chicken with bread sauce. An excellent game terrine can be made with pheasant breasts/ boned legs and an equal amount of coarsely minced belly of pork with usual seasonings – garlic, thyme, pepper, salt and, if you can get it, *Quatre Epices*.

Salmon

Traditionally, Salmon was poached but a big Salmon is not easy to poach on a home range. Baking in foil is simpler and can be done on a barbecue or in the oven. It is also a good way to do Sea trout. Cut foil with at least three inches extra at either end of fish. Butter foil generously (the fish will stick to unbuttered foil). Add fennel, celery, salt, peppercorns and half a glass of white wine. Wrap up and cook at 170°C (325°F, Mark 3) for 20 mins per 1lb (0.5kg). For sea trout 140°C, (275°F, Mark 1) for 30 mins per lb (0.5kg).

To barbecue, cook in foil not too close to the flame and roll over from time to time. About 15mins per 1lb (0.5kg).

Smoked Salmon

If you have a big Salmon it's often worth having it smoked. You can smoke a salmon which has been frozen. Have it sliced and packed in 100-200gm packs unless you need a whole side.

Traditional cold smoked Salmon is cured in salt and hung in a kiln over smouldering oak chips for several days. Fish merchants sometimes use chips from old whisky barrels. Home smokers are good for trout. Alternatively try Gravad Lax – place two raw salted fillets inside to inside with a bunch of dill and ground pepper sandwiched in between. Cover in foil. Weight lightly for two days. Slice.

'Coming South, Perth Station', 1895 by George Earl. Fashionable Victorians return south after the sporting season in Scotland. courtesy of the National Railway Museum, York.

Glossary

The most important word in Scottish Field Sports is 'piece'
– a snack or sandwich

SHOOTING

Bag — Total number of birds/animals for the day/period

Barker — A dog

Beater — Beats or flushes out birds

Bothy — Hut or shed often used for lunch

Brace — A pair, usually grouse or partridge

Burn — A small stream

Butt/Screen — A line of... enclosure for guns on grouse moor

Cheeper — Immature grouse

Covert — Woods/undergrowth for game

Decoy — Life-sized model of bird to lure in duck, pigeons or geese

Decoying — Shooting over decoys

Doo — Dialect for pigeon

Drive — Area walked through by beaters

Flanker — Beater on far outside of beating line

Flush — To rouse hidden game, also a flush (of birds)

Gun(s) — A person shooting, a shotgun

Hang — To hang game for period to improve flavour

Horn/whistle — Signal to stop shooting at end of a drive

Keeper — Professional in charge of game management

Mark — To note where bird or animal falls

Muirburn — Controlled burning of moorland

Over & under — Shotgun with barrels one on top of the other

Over! — Shouted warning of approaching bird

Peppered — Polite expression for shooting someone

Picker up — Dog handler whose dog picks up shot birds

Pluck & draw — Pull put bird feathers; draw out insides

Raptor — Bird of prey

Right & left — Two birds with two barrels

Rough shooting — Informal armed walk usually with dogs

Runner — Wounded bird

Running in — Dog out of control, running in to woods

Safety sticks — Sticks either side of grouse butt to limit swing

Shoot — Area of country used for shooting

Shot — A person who shoots, lead in a cartridge or sound of gun

Shotgun certificate Police licence to own shotgun – NOT rifle

Side by side Shotgun with barrels side by side

Stand or peg Numbered places/sticks on driven shoots

Stop Beater who stops birds sneaking out of a drive

Syndicate Group who share/rent sport-usually paid for.

The hill As in "going to the hill"; high moorland

Trap For catching vermin OR claypigeon launcher

Vermin Pests that damage wildlife or crops

Walked-up Shooting when quarry is flushed by walking guns

FISHING

Backing Reserve line attached to casting line

Beach/beaching Land a fish without net, see: grass

Beat Defined stretch of river

Bleeder Fish too damaged to return to river

Brownie Brown trout

Cast/leader Thin nylon at end of line to which a fly is tied

Cock Male salmon

Conehead Modern round-nosed fly

Croy/Groyne Rough stone pier to narrow improve pools/lies

Dapping Dancing a fly across surface of a loch

Day ticket Permit to fish for the day

Dry fly Floating fly

Fankle Tangle of cast or line

Finnock Young sea trout

Fly Hook dressed in specific colours of feather and fur

Fry Baby salmon

Gaff Long handled hook for landing fish (seldom used)

Ghillie Fishing guide often acts as keeper or stalker

Grass To Grass; have the fish safely on the bank

Grilse Salmon that returns after one winter at sea

Hatch Flies hatching on water surface

Hen Female salmon

Kelt Salmon in poor condition after spawning

Kipper Slang; red coloured salmon, suitable for smoking

Kype Lower hooked jaw of a male salmon

Lie	A particular spot where fish lie ie behind a boulder
Loch	Lake
Lochan	Small loch
Lure	Any device to lure a fish, not usually a fly
Mend	Flick or lift line straight as it lands on water
Parr	One year old salmon
Plug	American lure not much used for salmon
Pool	Where fish lie in a river or burn
Pump	Gentle heave on rod to tire hooked fish
Priest	Short heavy truncheon for killing fish
Rainbow (trout)	Non-native trout stocked in trout fisheries
Rawner/Baggott	Unspawned salmon
Redd	Shallow gravelly spawning area
Run	Fast bit of river; fish coming upstream together
Sea lice	Parasite which indicates fish is fresh from the sea
Sea loch	Loch open to sea
Sea trout	Migratory brown trout
Smolt	2-4 yr old salmon ready to go to sea for first time
Spate	Surge of river water

Spey cast	Rolling forward cast avoiding bank behind
Spinner	Spinning lure
Tailer	Long handled wire snare for landing fish by the tail
Trolling	'Trawling' a spinner behind boat
Tube fly	Fly tied on plastic or brass tube
Voe	Sea loch or inlet in Shetland
Waddington	Three inch long heavy feathered lure for deep fishing
Waders	Thigh or chest height waterproof boots; birds
Wading stick	Lead weighted stick (so it won't float away)
Wet fly	Sinking fly
Wrist	Narrowest part of a fish's fish body, at tail

STALKING

Argo (cat) Tracked vehicle to take deer off hill – or guests up the hill

Beast Deer

Beat Area or division of stalking ground

Bipod Short, two-legged rifle support to steady aim

Buck Male Roe or Fallow deer

Calf Young deer

Cleg Horsefly; to be avoided

Cull Selectively reducing deer numbers

Dead ground Area out of sight to deer

Doe Female Roe or Fallow deer

Firearm certificate Licence for rifle issued by police

Garron Highland pony for taking game off the hill

Glass Traditional word for telescope; also 'to glass'

Gralloch deer entrails; to remove entrails

Haunch Whole leg and buttock of a deer

Hind Female Red deer

Hummel Stag that has not grown antlers

Imperial/Monarch Stag with 14-point antlers

Medal head Classication; gold,silver, bronze, usually of Roe

Midge Insect, curse of the Highlands.

Pony boy Boy/man looking after stalking pony

Pizzle Stag's penis

Refuge Safe haven for deer

Royal Stag with 12-point antlers

Rut The mating period; to rut, to mate

Sound moderator Silencer for rifle to reduce recoil and noise

Spy Scan hill for deer usually with telescope

Stag Male Red deer

Stalk The act of creeping up on an animal

Stalker Professional deer manager who takes guests stalking

Stalking sticks Rifle support for standing shot

Switch Stag with antlers like spears, no tines

Ticks Insects whose bite causes Lyme disease in humans

Trophy head Antlers on head good enough to be mounted

Velvet Seasonal antler covering, cast off before rut

Venison Meat of any deer

Wee staggie! A small stag

Winded To be scented or heard by deer

Acknowledgements

A great many people have helped with this book. First and foremost I must thank Sally Duncanson of the Scottish Tour Guides Association for asking me if a book of this sort existed. It did not. It does now.

To all those friends who so kindly sent photographs, even though I could use only a fraction, many thanks. I could not have done without them.

In particular I'd like to thank Mel Shand from Finzean and Linda Mellor from North Fife both of whom made available the entire contents of their picture libraries, also Calum Campbell from Esslemont. Kirsten Scheuerl from Coupar was sweetly forbearing amidst all my curious demands (Have you got a ferret with a rabbit in its mouth?). Chris Hewitt and Peter Keyser took a great deal of trouble to get me the right pictures. Andrew Graham-Stewart produced some very special fishing and stalking pictures and much advice. Robbie Douglas-Miller enthusiastically clogged up my computer for two days with a stream of exceptional photographs. Robert Rattray of CKDGalbraith made encouraging noises and kept me right on a number of technical details.

For wading through the copy and pointing out serious howlers while offering gentle advice, I must thank Colin Shedden of BASC, Richard Cooke of the ADMG and John Bruce of the British Deer Society. I must also thank Pete Moore of SNH for his sure guidance and Victoria Brooks of the Scottish Country Sports Tourism Group for her help and enthusiasm.

I am particularly grateful to David Hawson who produced the wonderful illustrations all, apparently, while trying to catch a bus from Monymusk to Madrid.

For the design and layout and great forbearance in the face of endless chopping and changing on my part, I am eternally grateful to Fiona Hill of Finks Publishing, without whom this book would never have happened.

I have tried to meet copyright requirements by tracing photographers but in some cases this has proved impossible for which I apologise.